Great Ideas, Gentle as Doves

Great Ideas, Gentle as Doves

Second Edition

The Universal Apostolic Preferences
of the Society of Jesus Embrace
Catholic Social Teaching

Timothy Brown, S.J.

Apprentice
House Press
Loyola University Maryland

Second Edition

Paperback ISBN: 978-1-62720-611-2

Published by Apprentice House Press

Apprentice
House Press
Loyola University Maryland

Loyola University Maryland
4501 N. Charles Street, Baltimore, MD 21210
410.617.5265
www.ApprenticeHouse.com
info@ApprenticeHouse.com

Introduction

In assembling this selection of essays, prayers, and scripture passages, I hope to engage the reader in the vibrancy of Catholic Social Teaching. My thought was to collect these essays in one place and, through questions following each essay, provide the means for further reflection on these important topics.

At this point in our history, the rich tapestry of Catholic Social Teaching can provide a sense of direction in our lives. We all make up the fabric of life – woven together in a single cloth – and all are stewards of each other and creation as a whole.

The ideas that make up the body of Catholic Social Teaching are not new ideas. It is my hope that these selections will stimulate us to greater service to each other and to our world. That the world will begin to pay attention to this "faith flutter of wings," this "stirring of hope."

I have included reflections form Laudato Si as an introduction to my book. Integral Ecology teaches us that everything we value is closely interrelated. I value education. Especially to those on the margins. I value a care for our common home, I value the way in which we pray, reflect, and dialogue on the issues of our time. I hope this book inspires, challenges, and impels you to work for social justice.

"What is the purpose of our life in this world? ... What is the goal of our work and all our efforts? What need does the earth have of us?" In *Laudato Si'*, Pope Francis strives to answer the questions at the very heart of our existence. He says, "Unless we struggle with these deeper issues, I do not believe that our concern for ecology will produce significant results."

There are several themes that unify this encyclical. They are:

- the intimate relationship between the poor and the fragility of the planet
- the conviction that everything in the world is connected
- the critique of new forms of power derived from technology
- the call to seek other ways of understanding the economy and progress
- the "value proper to each creature" and the human meaning of ecology
- the need for forthright and honest debate
- the serious responsibility of international and local policy
- the throwaway culture and the proposal of a new lifestyle

This book chronicles some of my efforts to put those Gospel ideals into practice My hope is that these examples might inspire you to become a practitioner of Catholic Social teachings:

AMDG

- Ad Majorem Dei Gloriam
- To the greater glory of God. Our Jesuit motto
- Actualize my Divine Gifts
- How do you characterize your AMDG ?

How to ask the proper AMDG questions

- Ask the question: Why this injustice
- Ask the question: What can we change?
- Ask the question: Where does the Living Christ appear in this challenging scene of suffering and grief
- Ask the question: Where can we discover the God of hope in this challenging setting
- Ask the question: How do we together discern a possible climate change strategy ?
- Ask the question: What are some practical solutions to address the spiritual needs of those on the margins

The Universal Apostolic Preferences of the Society of Jesus

Dear friends in the Lord:

The Universal Apostolic Preferences, which I promulgate with this letter, are the fruit of an election. A choice has been made among several possibilities, all of them good. Our desire has been to find the best way to serve the Church at this time, the best contribution we can make with what we are and have, seeking to do what is for the greater divine service and the more universal good.

At the end of the sixteen months that the process lasted at the various levels of the Society, I presented to the Holy Father four universal apostolic preferences:

A. To show the way to God through the Spiritual Exercises and discernment;

B. To walk with the poor, the outcasts of the world, those whose dignity has been violated, in a mission of reconciliation and justice;

C. To accompany young people in the creation of a hope-filled future;

D. To collaborate in the care of our Common Home.

In his confirmation letter of 6 February 2019, Pope Francis observed that "the process that the Society followed to arrive at universal apostolic preferences was (…) a real discernment." He affirmed that the proposed preferences "are in agreement with the current priorities of the Church as expressed through the ordinary magisterium of the Pope, the Synods, and the Episcopal Conferences, especially since Evangelii gaudium."

The Holy Father insisted that "the first preference is crucial because it presupposes as a basic condition the Jesuit's relationship with the Lord in a personal and communal life of prayer and discernment." And he added: "Without this prayerful attitude the other preferences will not bear fruit."

A. To show the way to God through the Spiritual Exercises and discernment

We resolve to collaborate with the Church in experiencing secular society as a *sign of the times* that affords us the opportunity to renew our presence in the heart of human history.

We resolve to gain a deeper experience of the Spiritual Exercises.

We resolve to offer the Spiritual Exercises in as many ways as possible.

We resolve to promote discernment as a regular habit for those who choose to follow Christ.

We resolve to make regular use of spiritual conversation and discernment in our implementation of the preferences at all levels of the life-mission of the Society.

B. To walk with the poor, the outcasts of the world, those whose dignity has been violated, in a mission of reconciliation and justice

The necessary condition for becoming companions "on the way" in the style of Jesus is, out of closeness with the poor, "to announce his Gospel of hope to the many poor who inhabit our world today."

The path we seek to follow with the poor is one that promotes social justice and the change of economic, political, and social structures that generate injustice; this path is a necessary dimension of the reconciliation of individuals, peoples, and their cultures with one another, with nature, and with God.

We confirm our commitment to care for migrants, displaced persons, refugees, and victims of wars and human trafficking. We also resolve to defend the culture and the dignified existence of indigenous peoples.

We commit ourselves to help eliminate abuses inside and outside the Church.

Accompanying the impoverished requires us to improve our studies, our analysis, and our reflection in order to understand in depth the economic, political, and social processes that generate such great injustice; we must also contribute to the elaboration of alternative models.

C. To accompany the young in the creation of a hope-filled future

It is the young who, from their perspective, can help us to understand better the epochal change that we are living and its hope-filled newness.

The apostolic works of the Society of Jesus can make an important contribution to creating and maintaining spaces that are open to young people in society and the Church.

To accompany young people demands of us authenticity of life, spiritual depth, and openness to sharing the life-mission that gives meaning to who we are and what we do.

D. To collaborate in the care of our Common Home

We resolve, considering who we are and the means that we have, to collaborate with others in the construction of alternative models of life that are based on respect for creation and on a sustainable development capable of producing goods that, when justly distributed, ensure a decent life for all human beings on our planet.

Conversion for us, Jesuits and our companions in mission, begins by changing the habits of life promoted by an economic and cultural system based on the consumption of an irrational production of goods.

—Excerpts from *Universal Apostolic Preferences of the Society of Jesus, 2019-2029*
Arturo Sosa, S.I.
Superior General

Introducing the Universal Apostolic Preferences

On February 19, 2019, Fr. General Arturo Sosa announced the so-called Universal Apostolic Preferences for the Society. The organizers of this assembly have asked me to answer three questions about them: what they are, how they came about, and what Fr. General wants us to do with them. I'll use those questions as a structure, but I shall take the liberty of adding two others: what kind of faith and hope do they presuppose, and how are they encouraging us to re-imagine ourselves as Jesuit and Ignatian disciples.

What are they?

At the very simplest level, we are talking about four aspirations, four statements of intent and purpose:

A.   To show the way to God through the Spiritual Exercises and discernment;

B.   To walk with the poor, the outcasts of the world, those whose dignity has been violated, in a mission of reconciliation and justice;

C.   To accompany young people in the creation

of a hope-filled future;

D.   To collaborate in the care of our Common Home.

Even in official sources, the formulations, and also their order, differ a bit. But it's important to see them not as simple nouns (spirituality, ecology), but rather as phrases denoting action, phrases centered on verbs. In his letter promulgating the preferences, Fr. Sosa presented them as the culmination of an attempt 'to find the best way to collaborate in the Lord's mission, the best way to serve the Church at this time, the best contribution we can make with what we are and have, seeking to do what is for the greater divine service and the more universal good.' They set out a program for the next ten years.

-Philip Endean, S.J.

Wisdom 7:22-8:1

Wisdom, the fashioner of all things, taught me.
There is in her a spirit that is intelligent, holy,
unique, manifold, subtle,
mobile, clear, unpolluted,
distinct, invulnerable, loving the good,
keen, irresistible,
beneficent, humane, steadfast,
sure, free from anxiety,
all-powerful, overseeing all,
and penetrating through all spirits
that are intelligent, pure, and altogether subtle.
For wisdom is more mobile than any motion;
because of her pureness
she pervades and penetrates all things.
For she is a breath of the power of God,
and a pure emanation of the glory of the Almighty;
therefore nothing defiled gains entrance into her.
For she is a reflection of eternal light,
a spotless mirror of the working of God,
and an image of his goodness.
Although she is but one, she can do all things,
and while remaining in herself, she renews all things;
in every generation she passes into holy souls

and makes them friends of God, and prophets;
for God loves nothing so much
as the person who lives with wisdom.
She is more beautiful than the sun,
and excels every constellation of the stars.
Compared with the light she is found to be superior,
for it is succeeded by the night,
but against wisdom evil does not prevail.
She reaches mightily from one end of the earth to the other,
and she orders all things well.

In Days to Come

In days to come
    the mountain of the Lord's house
Shall be established as the highest of mountains,
    and shall be raised up above the hills.
Peoples shall stream to it,
    and many nations shall come and say:
"Come, let us go up to the mountain of the LORD,
    to the house of the God of Jacob;
    that he may teach us in his ways
    and that we may walk in his paths."
For out of Zion shall go forth instruction,
    and the word of the LORD from Jerusalem.
He shall judge between many peoples
    and shall arbitrate between strong nations far away;
    they shall beat their swords into plowshares,
    and their spears into pruning hooks;
    nation shall not lift up sword against nation
    neither shall they learn war any more;
    but they shall sit under their own vines
    and under their own fig trees,

and no one shall make them afraid;
for the mouth of the Lord of hosts has spoken.

— *Micah 4:1-4*

Part 1

To Show the Way to God through the
Spiritual Exercises and Discernment

Vision

Do you have a vision of God's call?

> "What does the Lord require of you but
> to do justice, and to love kindness, and to
> walk humbly with your God?"
>
> (Micah 6:8)

Do you have a vision of God's workers?

> "Let no one despise your youth, but set
> the believers an example in speech and
> conduct, in love, in faith, in purity."
>
> (1 Timothy 4:12)

Do you have a vision of God's people?

Do you have a vision of God's peace?

Do you have a vision of God's friendship?

Have you glimpsed God's vision?

Do you take seriously the words, "for it is in giving that we receive?"

Consciousness Examen

The mature Ignatius, near the end of his life, was always examining every movement and inclination of his heart, which means he was discerning the congruence of everything with his true Christ-centered self.

Our novice master, George Aschenbrenner, taught us how to pray, to discern, to practice the examen as a means to take stock throughout the day, a spiritual temperature. He would help us begin the lifelong practice of taking the hordes of images, impulses, dispositions, and moods, and allow them to become signals of the Spirit guiding us as young novices.

My novitiate takeaway, which stays with me to this very day, is the practice of distinguishing the three different dimensions of the interior life:

> First dimension: behavioral, external, observable, the superficial side

> Second dimension: the very real area of rational spontaneity, the skin of the soul

> Third dimension: the core of the soul, the deepest,

most profound identification with the Christ within the core of my being, my name of grace

How am I to be faithful to who I am at the core of my Jesuit identity as a novice in the Society of Jesus?

Once I got into the habit of working with the three dimensions of spiritual self, my Jesuit identity began to take hold.

"I have called you by your name. You are mine." – Isaiah 43

Looking out at the horizon from the front door – how many men and women have stood at that front door, looking at the horizon, a different horizon for each one of us. Our images of God were inspired by this landscape, formed by our times and culture, and encouraged by the Holy Spirit.

Each of us can name those who helped to form us – spiritual directors, fellow retreatants, novices, Jesuits. The names of our novice masters, the rectors of the community, the men who passed through these doors and lien now in the ground here, are a fitting litany of comfort and advocacy and sanctification, they were to us spirits of counsel and fortitude, of grace and prayer.

There is a wonderful poem by Sir Stephen Spender, *I Think Continually of Those Who Were Truly Great*. It begins:

I think continually of those who were truly great.
Who, from the womb, remembered the soul's history
Through the corridors of light where the hours are suns,

Endless and singing.

To name them in your heart and prayer together

I think of past novice masters:

> *John McEvoy*
> *Tom Gavigan*
> *Dom Maruca*
> *George Aschenbrenner*
> *Jim Maier*
> *Jim Conroy*

—George Aschenbrenner, S.J.

Paying Attention

I want to share with you a few thoughts regarding the role of service within the context of a Jesuit institution like Loyola College in Maryland. In the Contemplation of the Incarnation in the Spiritual Exercises, Saint Ignatius asks that we try to place ourselves with the Trinity, as they look down on the earth and behold persons in such great diversity in dress and manner of acting:

"Some are white, some black, some at peace, and some at war; some weeping, some laughing; some well, some sick; some coming into the world, and some dying."

I carry that image of attentiveness around with me as a way to put a perspective on service in the context of Loyola College. As a Jesuit institution, I believe our task is not only to give students the skills they need for distinguished professional performance but also to teach them to be leaders who are sensitive to justice and service and who can exercise their power with competence and compassion.

The Center for Values and Service was established to organize service outreach programs and to promote faith and education for justice through reflection and academic study. The Center strives to respond to the challenge of the leaders of our Jesuit schools issued by Peter-Hans Kolvenbach, the Superior General of the Society of Jesus, in a 1989 address. In the words of Fr. Kolvenbach: "We want graduates who will be leaders concerned about the society and the world in which they live, desirous of eliminating hunger and conflict in the world, sensitive to the need for more equitable distribution of God's bounty, seeking to end sexual and social discrimination, eager to share their faith and their love with others. In short, we want our graduates to be leaders in service." Moreover, "the service of faith through the promotion of justice…which is profoundly linked with our preferential option for the poor, [must] be operative in our lives and our institutions." To be faithful to this vision, college students — and universities themselves — must find creative ways to embrace this "preferential option for the poor" and the mandate for solidarity with people who are materially poor that it necessarily entails.

Education in service of the materially disadvantaged may, to some, seem quite radical. But, in many ways, it follows a long-standing tradition, especially in Jesuit history, rooted in a pedagogy that distinguishes true education from simple training. We go to school not so much for knowledge alone, but rather to develop virtuous habits: the habit of expression, the habit of attention, even the habit of being. Developing these habits of virtue requires an integrated effort that involves linking service experience with rigorous classroom study. It takes practice and even concentration. Most fundamentally it requires us to cultivate the habit of paying attention.

In *Waiting for God*, Simone Weil develops this theme of attentiveness in an essay entitled "Reflections on the Right School Studies with a View of the Love of God." In it she explains that, for the person pursuing studies with a view to the love of God, one's sole interest and real object must be to develop the faculty of attention. She views attention as a kind of waiting, watching, and suspended thought. The point of all this is to be open to receive truth. She is interested in developing an attitude, a habit of paying attention, which I see as absolutely essential for our students, for it is this habit of contemplative attentiveness that empowers students to re-imagine the world in which we live.

Paying attention in this way requires extraordinary discipline and concentration. The capacity to give one's attention to a sufferer (to someone in need) is a very rare and difficult habit to develop—almost a miracle—and nearly all those who think they have this capacity do not possess it. To give this kind of attention means being able to say to our neighbor: "What are you going through?" To be able to pay attention to another in a community service setting challenges a student to be open to the experiences of another and to ask, "What are you about?"

Our students come to us in need of developing this habit of critically reflective attentiveness. This is essential if they are to acquire the ability to re-imagine our world in ways that reflect the Gospel values of fidelity, gratitude, compassion, self-giving love, reconciliation, hospitality, simplicity of life, inclusiveness, and respect for the dignity of each human person. At Loyola, we have a special mission, a special calling. We are challenged to make it possible for each person to seek the mark of God in all creation. We are called to make a case not only for functional literacy but for moral literacy as well: To create and foster some moral energy, moral passion, moral intelligence which says that we all can be larger than ourselves and to be able to ask the questions that are so crucial for these times.

We need to be respectfully attentive to the transcendent values of each and every person that are revealed in our encounters and relationships with others in service. It is these encounters and relationships that serve to spark the critical development of imagination. Imagination is the capacity of our hearts and minds to see meaning beyond what is immediately evident; to stretch the limits of the obvious. It is the ability to make connections, to envision possibilities. If we are to grow in our ability to imagine new possibilities for constituting good lives and good communities, it is essential that we attentively enter together into relationships and conversations in which we can encounter the lived realities and imaginative visions of others.

Developing one's moral imagination goes hand in hand with developing the ability to pay attention— to make good decisions—to find meaning in what one does. The gift of imagination allows us to see the things that we sometimes miss because of our limited attention spans. Through service with people who are materially poor, many students have begun to develop a particular vision of how the world could possibly be re-imagined. The vision—the paying attention, the "seeing as"—is very much an exercise of imagination. To reformulate their vision, many students have had to let go of pre-conceived notions of how people think, act, and live out their lives. Through their service experiences, I have seen scores of students forced to suspend past notions and impressions of the people with whom they are working; they have come to a deeper seeing of the world. I have seen students return to campus challenged by serious social problems. They have come back to Loyola stunned, sometimes confused, often times without the words to express their frustrations. With stories, metaphors, vision, and prayerful, contemplative reflection on service, imagination can offer another kind of resource – a moral resource.

Jesuit education, at its best, forms students who are able to engage in just this sort of creative re-imagining of their experiences and the world in which they live and act. And community service plays a crucial role in this education of the moral imagination. Through our service experiences, all of us—students, faculty and members of the communities in which service takes the world of others in their otherness, and in the concreteness of their diverse experience—grow in our ability to re-imagine the world we share. We "are freed to go out of ourselves and live with others in friendship," a friendship that compels us to strive to create communities that reverence the dignity of all people.

Broken Cisterns

O Lord,
do not let us turn into "broken cisterns"
that can hold no water…
do not let us be so blinded by the enjoyment
of the good things of earth
that our hearts become insensible to the cry
of the poor,
of the sick, or orphaned children
and of those innumerable brothers and
sisters of ours
who lack the necessary minimum to eat,
to clothe their nakedness,
and to gather their family together under
one roof.

— Pope John XXIII

Project Mexico

For the past decade, a number of students from Loyola College in Baltimore, Maryland have been spending their January break in Tecate and Tijuana in an enormously successful venture called Project Mexico. Twenty-five of us spent ten days working on two construction projects: one at a Catholic boys' orphanage conducted by a remarkable group of Mexican nuns, the other in a relatively new area of Tijuana, where we helped build a kitchen-cafeteria at which children can receive one hot meal a day for about a dollar. The hope is that the cafeteria will serve as a community center for people to share goods, food, clothing, and friendship.

Here is how one student described Project Mexico: "The project is a way of opening our eyes and hearts to global realities. We begin, many of us, as young people without an understanding of the full scope of human existence. In Mexico, we discovered at first hand the hard fact of extreme poverty. But the greatest discovery experienced is the compassion and kindness within the human spirit."

An instance of "opening our eyes and hearts" to "the hard fact of extreme poverty" is the following. In Mexico last year, we visited a group of people in one of the colonias or "settlements." They have a tradition that on the feast of the Three Kings, the children prepare a Christmas pageant, which is very important to all the people. Imagine that the poor, simple, smiling children in this obscure Mexican village shared the same sense of wonder and joy over their baby Jesus as did the shepherds and Magi 2,000 years ago.

As we know from the Gospel of Luke, no true homage to the birth of Jesus would be complete without a manger scene, and here in this village the manger scene was key to the whole Three Kings celebration. All the children played their parts, from Mary and Joseph to the shepherds. The Three Wise Men, the innkeeper, and even the animals turned out to be the real thing. And a cat, some chickens, and a few stray dogs also helped to form the backdrop.

As you picture this scene, you must not forget that these children were, in a real sense, very poor. The makeshift costumes worn that day were thrown-away clothes, rags pieced together. As the pageant unfolded, the children began praying and singing, and crowding closer and closer to the baby Jesus. The baby was a tiny creature a few months old, a beautiful baby boy clothed in rags. The other *niños* were practically on top of the child. I looked at the dirty ground, the animals sidling up to the infant, and then it struck me: this child – poor, dressed in rags, nearly helpless – he was the baby Jesus. This was probably truer to the actual setting and circumstances into which Jesus was born than any I had ever experienced. And that day I learned more about the reality of God's trusting love, his giving his son over to the world and to Mary.

Of my last Project Mexico experience I have several vivid, recurring recollections. One is of a small boy who dreamed of becoming an architect. Although I cannot remember his name, I am still troubled by the thought of him. I admired his sense of the future. In Mexico, the peoples' daily struggles with poverty and despair leave very little time for dreams. The fact that this boy could fancy such a future was a testimonial to the *madres* who reared him. But there was no real opportunity for him to see his dream reach fruition, and this realization frustrated me. Most boys do not even attend high school because their parents cannot afford the uniforms that the schools require.

Perspectives

Such hopes can be built on gratitude. There is an ancient Aztec prayer that speaks of gratitude and the preciousness of life and its fleetingness. As the Aztecs thank their God for their life, they acknowledge that they are simply on loan to one another for a short time. They have a prayer that reads:

Oh, only for so short a while
You have lent us to each other,
Because we take form in your act
of drawing us.
And we take life in your painting us,
And we breathe in your singing us.
But only for so short a while

Have you lent us to each other.

Isn't seeing life as being on loan a great philosophy to hold? I think it helps us to be courageous, to take risks, to be adventurous and daring. When you look at life as being on loan, you look at things differently. You look at this loan for what it really is – a pure gift, pure grace given to us from God. When you look at life as a loan, material things are put into perspective.

I once heard a wise Jesuit say that it is impossible to be grateful and unhappy at the same time. When I was in Mexico last January I understood what he meant, and can remember hearing some Loyola students from that trip make similar observations. Two students of the group met Lupe and her son Federico while volunteering at La Casa de los Pobres (House of the Poor), in Tijuana. There, needy people can receive two meals a day, groceries, clothing, and health care. During their time at the Casa, the students became close to Lupe and Federico. On their last night in Tijuana, before joining the rest of us in Tecate, they gave Federico a small bag of toys and money. But when they took him home that evening, Federico showed them an act of generosity and selflessness that few might expect from a seven-year-old. As soon as the little boy got into the house, he took the bag and the money and gave them to his mother to divide among the other children. That's the way every-one was. They help others before they help themselves. The philosophy of all being on loan seems to have taken place in that situation.

Another student who graduated last May had her own special story of a woman who deeply touched her. Lupita is the mother of Gustavo and Martín, two boys from the orphanage where we worked. They stayed at the orphanage because Lupita was too poor and sick to care for them. Lupita lived in one of the poorest *colonias* in Tijuana, where people attempt to survive in structures made of plastic, cardboard, tires, or whatever else they can find. Part of Project Mexico's money that year went toward the construction of a new house for Lupita and her family. A woman in her 50s, Lupita has to travel down a steep hill to get water for cleaning and cooking and despite her cancer, arthritis, and high blood pressure, she must then carry the huge jugs back up the steep slope. When the small group of Loyola students went to visit Lupita for the first time, she greeted them with hugs, invited them into her house, and prepared tea and coffee for them. She had little to offer but gave what little she had. That kind of hospitality made a deep impression on the students.

On January 3, another group will leave for Mexico. They are able to make the trip because of the generosity and assistance of many people at Loyola. The support for this venture has been tremendous. I think it can be said that Loyola College has demonstrated a gratitude and appreciation which mirrors that displayed by the Mexican people. "What you receive as a gift – give as a gift!"

After returning from their trip to Mexico over one Christmas break, students wrote down their impressions and reflections. Here are excerpts from the paper of a young man who had made the trip:

"What an amazing day! We started off going to Leander, a colonia in Tijuana, and we were to build a kindergarten building. It is so poor here, yet they have nothing but incredible love and peace with themselves. We did various activities such as construct a bathroom, put it over the septic tank, and dig ditches for people."

Change the World

"You can never teach anyone something – you can only help them find it within themselves. After Mass, we spent the time talking and mixing cultures and friendship. Peace and love are given so easily by the Mexicans, and their hospitality is overwhelming... We talked to some migrants; in their reflections people spoke about being frustrated at the lack of work... Everyone was sad about what we have in comparison to them and about why they cannot get ahead. It ended on a note that it is in our hands to educate ourselves and others and to never forget what we saw. Never doubt that a small group of thoughtful, committed persons can help change the world."

"Sunday I went to an old age home run by Mother Teresa's Missionaries of Charity... We had several jobs to do here such as cleaning, feeding the handicapped, doing laundry by hand. I gave people manicures and pedicures with nail clippers. It was really not like work because there is such self-satisfaction in doing it."

"Day nine at the orphanage. We slept through the night, our next to last, listening to the windows slam and the rain pour down on Rancho Nazareth. Not even the rain, however, could hinder us totally from our tasks at hand that we wanted to finish. The roofers were desperately trying to patch all the holes, the painters groomed, and those working on the fence around the garden forgot the wind and rain to accomplish their goal. They desired to give every last effort. Time with the boys was very special before we left. It was starting to get sad, and grins were turning into faces of sorrow. Both sides of the border felt the pain that would come with our departure the next morning. But we shrugged it off until then. The next day we left. The bus drove down the hill."

"Looking back, we watched the boys run after the bus and catch their last glimpse. I can't write down all the thoughts and reactions of the last ten days. It is too incredible. Words are not enough… God bless the people of Mexico."

While I Was Still Young

While I was still young, before I went on my travels,
I sought wisdom openly in my prayer.
Before the temple I asked for her,
and I will search for her until the end.

From the first blossom to the ripening grape
my heart delighted in her;
my foot walked on the straight path;
from my youth I followed her steps.

I inclined my ear a little and received her,
and I found for myself much instruction.
I made progress in her;
to him who gives wisdom I will give glory.

For I resolved to live according to wisdom,
and I was zealous for the good,
and I shall never be disappointed.
My soul grappled with wisdom,
and in my conduct I was strict;

I spread out my hands to the heavens,
and lamented my ignorance of her.

I directed my soul to her,
and in purity I found her.

With her I gained understanding from the first;
therefore I will never be forsaken.
My heart was stirred to seek her;
therefore I have gained a prize possession.
The Lord gave me my tongue as a reward,
and I will praise him with it.

Draw near to me, you who are uneducated,
and lodge in the house of instruction.
Why do you say you are lacking in these things,
and why do you endure such great thirst?
I opened my mouth and said,
Acquire wisdom for yourselves without money.
Put your neck under her yoke,
and let your souls receive instruction;
it is to be found close by.

— Sirach 51:13–26

I think we ought to read only books that bite and sting us. If the book we are reading doesn't shake us awake like a blow to the skull, why bother reading it in the first place? So that it can make us happy, as you put it? Good God, we'd be just as happy if we had no books at all; books that make us happy, we could, in a pinch, also write ourselves. What we need are books that hit us like a most painful misfortune, like the death of someone we loved more than we love ourselves, that make us feel as though we had been banished to the woods, far from any human presence, like a suicide. A book must be the ax for the frozen sea within us. That is what I believe.

— Franz Kafka

Reading, Fitting the Pieces of a Puzzle

I believe that the art of reading and re-reading is a creative way of puzzling together the words on the page and designing. To take all the scattered pieces of information and imagery, metaphors, and poetry - to put the pieces of the puzzle together - is the great contemplative moment. To take all the scattered pieces of information, data, detailed accounts, and descriptions and organize them into patterns and shapes and figures in a very slow and methodical way is Jesuit education at its best. To connect the core – philosophy to history, literature to theology – and all the social sciences in between is an artistic practice. To take one's time to piece together slowly and thoroughly is to open the mind to wonder and imagination and inquiry, all aspects of Jesuit pedagogy.

Slow reading — never skipping a word or a sentence — watching how the sentences develop into paragraphs and into fully thought through images. The invisible becoming visible in the mind of the reader.

The secret to slow reading — the opportunity to decelerate,

to take the time to ponder and muse, and all the surprises that come when the puzzle pieces come together.

Attentive pauses and the ultimate discovery that attention is the natural prayer of the soul.

That love is from God and of God towards God that circle of love – the ideal end point of Jesuit learning.

I read somewhere that it is impossible to interrupt a book

— just yourself. That uninterrupted slow reading that brings a peace of mind that cannot be robbed.

Slowing down...

The fun of slowly putting the pieces together...

In Praise of Reading
and Fiction

I learned to read at the age of five, in Brother Justiniano's class at the De la Salle Academy in Cochabamba, Bolivia. It is the most important thing that has ever happened to me. Almost seventy years later I remember clearly how the magic of translating the words in books into images enriched my life, breaking the barriers of time and space and allowing me to travel with Captain Nemo twenty thousand leagues under the sea, fight with d'Artagnan, Athos, Portos, and Aramis against the intrigues threatening the Queen in the days of the secretive Richelieu, or stumble through the sewers of Paris, transformed into Jean Valjean carrying Marius's inert body on my back.

Reading changed dreams into life and life into dreams and placed the universe of literature within reach of the boy I once was. My mother told me the first things I wrote were continuations of the stories I read because it made me sad when they concluded or because I wanted to change their endings. And perhaps this is what I have spent my life doing without realizing it: prolonging in time, as I grew, matured, and aged, the stories that filled my childhood with exaltation and adventures.

If in this address I were to summon all the writers to whom I owe a few things or a great deal, their shadows would plunge us into darkness. They are innumerable. In addition to revealing the secrets of the storytelling craft, they obliged me to explore the bottomless depths of humanity, admire its heroic deeds, and feel horror at its savagery. They were my most obliging friends, the ones who vitalized my calling and in whose books I discovered that there is hope even in the worst of circumstances, that living is worth the effort if only because without life we could not read or imagine stories.

At times I wondered whether writing was not a solipsistic luxury in countries like mine, where there were scant readers, so many people who were poor and illiterate, so much injustice, and where culture was a privilege of the few. These doubts, however, never stifled my calling, and I always kept writing even during those periods when earning a living absorbed most of my time. I believe I did the right thing, since if, for literature to flourish, it was first necessary for a society to achieve high culture, freedom, prosperity, and justice, it never would have existed. But thanks to literature, to the consciousness it shapes, the desires and longings it inspires, and our disenchantment with reality when we return from the journey to a beautiful fantasy, civilization is now less cruel than when storytellers began to humanize life with their fables. We would be worse than we are without the good books we have read, more conformist, not as restless, more submissive, and the critical spirit, the engine of progress, would not even exist. Like writing, reading is a protest against the insufficiencies of life. When we look in fiction for what is missing in life, we are saying, with no need to say it or even to know it, that life as it is does not satisfy our thirst for the absolute – the foundation of the human condition – and should be better. We invent fictions in order to live somehow the many lives we would like to lead when we barely have one at our disposal.

Without fictions we would be less aware of the importance of freedom for life to be livable, the hell it turns into when it is trampled underfoot by a tyrant, an ideology, or a religion. Let those who doubt that literature not only submerges us in the dream of beauty and happiness but alerts us to every kind of oppression, ask themselves why all regimes determined to control the behavior of citizens from cradle to grave fear it so much they establish systems of censorship to repress it and keep so wary an eye on independent writers. They do this because they know the risk of allowing the imagination to wander free in books, know how seditious fictions become when the reader compares the freedom that makes them possible and is exercised in them with the obscurantism and fear lying in wait in the real world. Whether they want it or not, know it or not, when they invent stories the writers of tales propagate dissatisfaction, demonstrating that the world is badly made and the life of fantasy richer than the life of our daily routine. This fact, if it takes root in their sensibility and consciousness, makes citizens more difficult to manipulate, less willing to accept the lies of the interrogators and jailers who would like to make them believe that behind bars they lead more secure and better lives.

Since every period has its horrors, ours is the age of fanatics, of suicide terrorists, an ancient species convinced that by killing they earn heaven, that the blood of innocents washes away collective affronts, corrects injustices, and imposes truth on false beliefs. Every day, all over the world, countless victims are sacrificed by those who feel they possess absolute truths. With the collapse of totalitarian empires, we believed that living together, peace, pluralism, and human rights would gain the ascendancy and the world would leave behind holocausts, genocides, invasions, and wars of extermination. None of that has occurred. New forms of barbarism flourish, incited by fanaticism, and with the proliferation of weapons of mass destruction, we cannot overlook the fact that any small faction of crazed redeemers may one day provoke a nuclear cataclysm. We have to thwart them, confront them, and defeat them. There aren't many, although the tumult of their crimes resounds all over the planet and the nightmares they provoke overwhelm us with dread. We should not allow ourselves to be intimidated by those who want to snatch away the freedom we have been acquiring over the long course of civilization. Let us defend the liberal democracy that, with all its limitations, continues to signify political pluralism, coexistence, tolerance, human rights, respect for criticism, legality, free elections, alternation in power, everything that has been taking us out of a savage life and bringing us closer – though we will never attain it – to the beautiful, perfect life literature devises, the one we can deserve only by inventing, writing, and reading it. By confronting homicidal fanatics we defend our right to dream and to make our dreams reality.

From the cave to the skyscraper, from the club to weapons of mass destruction, from the tautological life of the tribe to the era of globalization, the fictions of literature have multiplied human experiences, preventing us from succumbing to lethargy, self-absorption, resignation. Nothing has sown so much disquiet, so disturbed our imagination and our desires as the life of lies we add, thanks to literature, to the one we have, so we can be protagonists in the great adventures, the great passions real life will never give us. The lies of literature become truths through us, the readers transformed, infected with longings and, through the fault of fiction, permanently questioning a mediocre reality. Sorcery, when literature offers us the hope of having what we do not have, being what we are not, acceding to that impossible existence where like pagan gods we feel mortal and eternal at the same time, that introduces into our spirits non-conformity and rebellion, which are behind all the heroic deeds that have contributed to the reduction of violence in human relationships. Reducing violence, not ending it. Because ours will always be, fortunately, an unfinished story.

That is why we have to continue dreaming, reading, and writing, the most effective way we have found to alleviate our mortal condition, to defeat the corrosion of time, and to transform the impossible into possibility.

—Mario Vargas Llosa
Excerpts from Nobel Lecture
7 December 2010
Swedish Academy, Stockholm

Part 2

To Walk with the Poor, the Outcasts of the World, those whose Dignity has been Violated, in a Mission of Reconciliation and Justice

If you bring your gift to the altar and there recall that
your brother or sister has anything against you
Leave your gift
Leave it

Go first
Be reconciled
And then come back
Those are Jesus's words to you

Ask God for strength
The grace will follow

I heard a spiritual director say one time that
forgiving does not mean putting the other one on
    probation
No
God's way is bilateral not unilateral
Two sided
Reconciliation is a two way street

Inmates' Reflections – Jessup Correctional Institution

In addition to my responsibilities at Loyola, I am a volunteer instructor in the Jessup Prison Scholars Program, which offers non-credit college-level instruction at Jessup Correctional Institution in Maryland. There I teach courses in the area of law and business, law and society, law and spirituality, and sports law. Professor Drew Leder in the Philosophy department introduced me to the program, and I have been teaching there since 1995, with a sabbatical during the years I served as provincial of the Maryland Province of the Society of Jesus.

One afternoon I shared with my Loyola students a book of reflections that I wrote several years ago entitled Great Ideas, Gentle as Doves: Reflections on Catholic Social Teachings. We discussed the rationale for the importance of university education in the prison setting. I pointed out the Universal Declaration of Human Rights, which states that "Everyone has the right to an education," and that "Education shall be directed to the full development of the human personality and to the strengthening of respect for human rights and fundamental freedoms," among other important tenets of the rights of every individual to participate in community life. In our reflection, I asked the class: How can you make this document a living reality at Jessup? How does this Declaration call you to assume a role in protecting the dignity of human life? What in this document inspires you to action? One student wrote:

> *Education is even more valued in the prison system because it allows a man for maybe the first time to understand and appreciate himself and see the beauty and importance of having and possessing the qualities of dignity, integrity, and honor that are acquired through hard work and determination to succeed. It is a tool that can uplift a man's self-esteem and give him the opportunity to understand and appreciate the joy of being respected for his ability to do something worthwhile and beneficial for himself and his family. It also serves as a positive social tool, which allows a man or a woman to get away from the mental and emotional psychosis of the prison environment and develop the proper social etiquette that is needed in positive, constructive, and productive environments.*

At Jessup, I often ask students to reflect on passages from the Bible. To illustrate the truth in the reflection by the Loyola student, following are some selected reflections on Psalm 62 by two of my students at Jessup. These reflections (shown in italics) remind us of the healing power of education and call us to recognize the dignity in all human beings.

2   My soul rests in God alone,
    from whom comes my salvation.
3   God alone is my rock and salvation,
    my fortress; I shall never fall.

Father Brown obviously thinks that "Restorative Justice" is possible. Of course, he doesn't say he can restore justice. Humility and pragmatism prevent him from making lofty or supercilious claims. He simply comes into this maximum security prison, each week, and teaches a course that begs for moral clarity.

When I think about Father Brown and our class, I am remind[ed] of a Zen story:

When Bankei held his seclusion weeks of meditation, pupils from many parts of Japan came to attend. During one of these gatherings a pupil was caught stealing. The matter was reported to Bankei with the request that the culprit be expelled. Bankei ignored the case.

Later the pupil was caught in a similar act, and again Bankei disregarded the matter. This angered the other pupils, who drew up a petition asking for the dismissal of the thief, stating that otherwise they would leave in a body.

When Bankei had read the petition he called everyone before him. "You are wise brothers," he told them. "You know what is right and what is wrong. You may go somewhere else to study if you wish, but this poor brother does not even know right from wrong. Who will teach him if I do not? I am going to keep him here even if all the rest of you leave."

A torrent of tears cleansed the face of the brother who had sto-
len. All desire to steal had vanished.

We inmates taking the course offered by Father Brown gen-
erally approached the law as we did life, from an adversarial
perspective. We stand guilty (convicted) of some very serious,
heinous even, offenses (murder, rape, armed robbery, etc.). It
would not, from a seemingly practical perspective, behoove any
one of us to acknowledge that he has committed a wrong and
must account for it. Our respective situations demand that we
claim that we were wronged [legally, socially, and/or morally].

—Arlando "Tray" Jones III

7   God alone is my rock and my salvation,
      my fortress; I shall not fall.

8   My deliverance and honor are with God,
      my strong rock;
      my refuge is with God.

Forgiveness is the largest spiritual and philosophical question
that challenges me. It shamelessly reveals my tendency toward
hypocrisy. On the one hand, I seek forgiveness for the many
wrongs that I've committed. While on the other hand, I find
it quite difficult to forgive the wrongs that have been commit-
ted against me. I often tell myself that there are some acts for
which there can be no expiration – no forgiveness. Of course,
if I accept that there are some acts for which forgiveness is not
possible, then I condemn myself to a psychological hell.

Long ago, I learned about the ABC system: "A" stands for activating event, "B" stands for belief system, and "C" is for emotional consequence. "A" never causes "C", the emotional consequence. "B" causes or directly leads to "C". In short, our belief about an activating event ("A") is what causes our emotional consequence ("C") – our feelings. For instance, if someone steals my watch, and I become angry about the thief, it's not the stealing of my watch, per se, that has me angry. It's my belief that I own the watch; it's my personal property and no one is supposed to take it without my permission. That is what has made me angry.

I face a great number of small, petty, nuisance stuff. But no one or nothing is big enough or significant enough to make me hate. I stand on the principle of forgiveness not because I'm some grand magnanimous person. I stand on it because I'm small and insignificant. Forgiveness simply props me up and carries me along my arduous journey sans the burden of hatred, resentment, and bitterness.

—Arlando "Tray" Jones III

10   Mortals are a mere breath,
       the sons of man but an illusion;
       On a balance they rise;
       together they weigh nothing.

For close to twenty years, I have experienced your passion for teaching men who are incarcerated and your compassion towards them. The first time we met, you were observing a philosophy course taught by Drew Leder in the Maryland Penitentiary. At the time, the penitentiary was a maximum security prison. *The class heard that you were an important person that would determine if the course would continue. Not long after, you started teaching business law there, and I became one of your students. In all the years I have taken your classes there are three things that you have emphasized: precise language, clear and logical reasoning, and eloquent writing. I am still working on the precise language and eloquent writing, but the logical reasoning I believe I have grasped. I always look forward to seeing you and taking your course, because I know I will learn something that will help me become a better human being.*

—John Woodland

Jesuit Education and Its Influence in the Prison System

I have been taking classes on law instructed by Father Tim Brown for approximately the past year. The Law is the written word of society having a conversation with itself, it demonstrates how the law makers and breakers adjust and readjust words, views and beliefs to accommodate their position and power. I believe that every group (religious or other) represents itself as an answer or solution to a problem or problems. I except the fact that a Jesuit education has influenced my life and made an impact on how I see myself, especially for the better.

A spiritual depth is the way of turning a symbol into substance, to reach beyond the call of basic formalities and join faith and work together. It takes a serious commitment to offer a wisdom to the downtrodden or relegated useless in our society (the prisoner). This is the compassion I see Father Tim Brown displaying whenever he visits us at Jessup Correctional Institution. To give something a spirit is to give it life and life symbolizes power. So I get power from being breathed on by the wisdom, knowledge and understanding about life from a teacher who is named Father Tim Brown.

Spiritual discernment is one, having the ability to recognize the truth and two, gaining some insight into what's important for the soul. I am prisoner so, I accept that I need to qualify those two areas in order to gain a better grip on who I am and what I need to do to make my situation better. Taking a look at my attraction to the worldly (negative or evil) things has allowed me to succumb to a way of habitually and practically committing chaotic acts on self and others that has relegated me to a beast level.

These are a few of the things that being a part of getting a Jesuit Education has allowed me to encounter. Self Improvement is the basis for community development and I am learning to place my desires below the communities desire to flourish and give meaning for it citizens. So, making a real contribution and making an effective impact is what it's really all about.

—Jessup student

9.1.2010

Dear Father Tim Brown:

I would like to begin by thanking you very much for everything you have done for all your students here at JCI. I believe that this is the opinion of the rest of the class including myself. For me it is a great honor to get to meet you, and get to know you. I also enjoy very much your excellent teaching style, your positive attitude, your humility, humbleness, and above all your sincere humanity. In addition, to your willingness to give unconditionally.

To me this represents not only a man who is devoted to education, especially for the disadvantaged people, incarcerated in the jail system, but also your willingness to help and give without expecting anything in return. This shows a caliber of a unique person whose only mission I goal is to help others.

To me this only represents a nobility in every aspect of it. Your teaching style not only is helping all of us, but personally it will stay me for the rest of my life, the following are some of it:

1. *In the beginning of the class, "I know some of you read and study law during incarceration, my advice to you today is to leave all this at the door and let us start from scratch."*

2. *"Law is like languages [German, French, English, Spanish, Arabic] you need.to learn it from scratch."*

3. *"The mind is an incredible gift. I am big on*

memorizing."

4. *"You need to read with your pen, you need to underline while reading."*

5. *"Doing Tort cases, leave your emotions at the door."*

6. *"The power of words in a contract, one word can help or destroy a contract."*

7. *"Remember the mirror rule for contracts, [offer, acceptance]."*

8. *"We need to meditate on this particular article."*

9. *"No court in the world would endorse a contract of drugs or life."*

And here are some quotes from the book you just provided us with last week which are extremely valuable:

1. *"Paying attention requires extraordinary discipline and concentration. The capacity to give one's attention to a sufferer [someone in need] is a very rare and difficult habit to develop... our students come to us in need of developing this habit of critically reflective attentiveness."*

2. *"We are free to go out of ourselves and live with others in friendship. A friendship that compels us to strive to create communities that reverence the dignity of all people."*

3. *"It is impossible to be grateful and unhappy at the same time.*

4. *"Education makes people decidedly human, it will enable them to take in their hands their own destinies, and bring about communities which are truly human."*

—Jessup student

As a convict for the past 21 years I am forever trying to learn. This is paramount to my "rehabilitation." No one is doing it for me. While doing this I am using my brain for future use. That is the objective I believe of this class / project.

The objective of any class to me is to teach, discuss / debate, test the minds of the students. How that student learns, acquires, retains knowledge varies and is up to the individual. Homework, as it's called, allows the student the opportunity to view all classroom material so that the individual can 'memorize' or retain paperwork, etc.

Father Brown is very smart in his teaching methods. He could also teach courses on criminal law. Perhaps this would be considered for future consideration.

We all would like the opportunity to be free. If we are not all afforded this opportunity, then please allow us to use our minds. This will give us the opportunity to feel "worth something" in this world. Perhaps if we receive our freedom we can return the favor by returning here or somewhere else and sharing this knowledge.

While they say knowledge is free I understand funds are needed to produce this course. I implore you to assist in procuring these funds. Convicts such as myself and many others are eager to learn. Don't judge us just on what occurred 10, 20, 30 years ago. For some they were innocent. It's not man's job to judge others. It's his job to help build up and better his fellowman. As a "traveling man" I live by this daily.

This opportunity has been a true blessing to me psyche. My mental faculties have been reborn. I am now rededicated to learning. For a convict this is Nirvana!! Without this many may cease to exist within themselves.

As an individual who is shunned, spit upon, etc. this is and should be a high-priority for further and expanded study.

We look forward to meeting new instructors teaching new things, new ideas. All I ask is to be given more opportunities of your generosity to learn.

1. *Education has always been the tool that has broadened the perspective of life of anyone who has seriously taken on the adventure and scholastic journey. It is even more valued in the prison system because it allows a man for maybe the first time to understand and appreciate himself and see the beauty and importance of having and possessing the qualities of dignity, integrity and honor that are acquired through hard work and determination to succeed. It is a tool that can uplift a man's self-esteem and give him the opportunity to understand and appreciate the joy of being respected for his ability to do something worthwhile and beneficial for himself and his family. It also serve as a positive social tool which allows a man or woman to get away from the mental and emotional psychosis of the prison environment and develop the proper social etiquettes that are needed in positive, constructive and productive environment.*

Unfortunately, some people felt that to finance the education of people who had committed an offense against society was morally and socially wrong. How could this be? Isn't it taught in the Education systems all of the world that "If a person wants to increase their understanding, appreciation and value for their own life, others and the world they live in that a good and proper education would do that. Would it not be the responsibility of those who understand the value of such a tool to present it to a person who has in the past showed socially and morally unacceptable behavior? I would think so, especially if 85% of these same people will return to society."

Education for me has been a mental, emotional and spiritual sanctuary. And for all the men that I have had the privilege to travel the halls of education within these prisons walls It has been a God sent mercy and a world of mental, emotional and spiritual suffering. All of their lives have improved as a result of it and their thirst for continued knowledge has been increased. It is my hope as well as their hope that more programs such as the one that Professor Tim Brown is giving is added to this environment in the near future. It can be not only a benefit to this environment but it will produce more mentally, emotionally and spiritually well balance human beings who will return back to society one day!

2. *There is plenty of work that is part and parcel of attending Father Brown's class. We are constantly being challenged to apply our reading and lecture material to real life cases. You are never safe from being called on, so you have to take the responsibility to perform the tasks assigned to you; namely*

*homework. As I have stated above, there is much
more to be learned than just the material that is
being taught. I was never a responsible student;
always procrastinating and ignoring obligations
in school. Comfortably floating along through the
semester and cramming the night before exams
was commonplace in my studies. Now, older and
a little wiser, I see the errors of my previous ways.
I see that my study habits also transgressed into
bad habits and choices in life, many involving
the continued use of drugs. They say hindsight is
20/20, but what good does that moment of clarity
do an individual unless they can apply it in the
present.*

*I was given that opportunity when I began attending Father
Brown's class. I am building responsible study habits that are a
direct result of the combination of Father Brown's teaching and
my new attitude. This is not a class that you can merely squeak
by on. I think that is a very important lesson regarding being
responsible in life. You may be able to make it on mediocrity for
a short time, but eventually your actions (or lack of) will cause
you more trouble than you can comprehend. I can honestly say
for the first time in my life, I want to do my assigned work.
More importantly the reason I want to be responsible is not
because I am afraid to let Father Brown down (a small part
I will admit though…), more importantly I am sick of letting
myself down. I have met many people in jail who are very
intelligent, interesting people. They just lacked the persistence
and responsibility the first time around. Does that mean that*

they are a lost cause? I refuse to believe so for my own sake. Responsibility is learned in baby steps. This is a small step for me to take toward the goal of returning to society as a productive member.

I can only hope that this class is used as a model to help inmates who want to help themselves. Many of us, myself included, are simply people who have made mistakes in life. Isn't the goal of incarceration to rehabilitate people and help them return to society and live a life free of criminal behavior? In order to allow people to return to society as productive members we need to provide them with outlets to effectuate personal, intellectual, and spiritual development. I write this from the perspective of one who has experience in this system. These words that are being typed as a review of the class is a testament to the personal development that is taking place within Father Brown's business law class at JCI. Hopefully, our class is not the only class that is able to experience something as positive as this.

3.   *In prison, very seldom do I have the opportunity to spread my wings and expand my horizon. Prison is a daily mundane routine. I wake up in the morning and go to work, or go into the yard to exercise. After I am finish, I take a shower, and walk to lunch. The rest of the day I am free to my own device: reading, watching television, or listening to music. This is my routine 7 days of the week, 365 days of the year, 27 years and counting.*

So it is refreshing as spring, and fulfilling as a full meal course to participate in an academic pursuit. When I attend classes offered by Loyola College and taught by Drew Leder and Father Tim Brown, I am inspired to embrace life. It also presents me with the opportunity to look at a different perspective. In these classes, I step out of the limited and restrictive confines of prison. For a period of time, I am free. I am able to explore. I am a student analyzing information in a critical manner. I am a person expressing my thoughts to my peers. The experience is enlightening.

I have been attending these classes with Drew and Father Tim, for over 15 years. I first met Drew at the Maryland Penitentiary. He was giving a seminar in philosophy. He exposed the group to ancient Greek philosophers: Epictetus, Plato, and Socrates. From there we investigated philosophys from around the world: Taoism, Buddhism, Sufism, and Yoruba animism. Drew has a Socratic method of teaching. He assigns a reading and draws the class into an energetic discussion. He then guides the glass through a lively debate. By asking members to give example of how their views affect their lives. He has help me become a critical thinker. My new approach to thinking has improved my life.

Father Tim teaching method is quite different from Drew's. He is precise and demanding. He assigns a reading and expects the class to be prepare to discuss every aspect of it. A student must be energetic and sharp to maintain his pace. He wants the class to thoroughly examine the law. He started our class off with a discussion o the United States Constitution. From there, we moved on to analyzing case law. We did this by dissecting the facts of the case. Then, we discussed the issue before the court.

Next, we scrutinized the court's reasoning and holding. During this time, Father Tim will stand in the front of the class urging us to think. I leave his class exhausted. He has help me recognize the importance of the law in making every day decisions. Both men have shown me the value of an education.

—Jessup student

Shortly before her untimely death of cancer, Sister Thea Bowman, evangelist, author, and teacher, was asked what her images of God were and how they had changed over the years. Her response sheds light on the impact of naming experiences:

> "I was reared in the traditional black community — in song and prayer and conversation and stories. My people graced me with multiple images of the living God.
>
> God is bread when you're hungry, water when you're thirsty, a harbor from the storm. God is a father to the fatherless, a mother to the motherless. God's my sister, my brother, my leader, my guide, my teacher, my comforter, my friend. God's the way-maker and burden-bearer, a heart-fixer and a mindregulator. God's my doctor who never lost a patient, my lawyer who never lost a case, my chaplain who never lost a battle. God's my all in all, my everything.
>
> God's my rock, my sword, my shield, my lily of the valley, my pearl of great price. God's a God of peace and a God of war. Counselor, Emmanuel, Redeemer, Savior, Prince of Peace, Son of God, Mary's little baby, wonderful Word of God."

These images come from Scripture and from the meditations of Christians. Some people see them as contradictory, but Christians see them as inadequate — all of them. But all these images are available to me. I meditate on each one of these images on a particular day at a particular time. Each one corresponds to a particular need. All these images help me as I call upon God's name.

—U.S. Catholic, April 1990

Part 3

To Accompany the Young in the
Creation of a Hope-filled Future

So as my understanding of God evolves, so too, my under-standing of myself and the call to the priesthood takes on new meaning. This new understanding of God as life-giver gives a special meaning to the work — developing self-respect in others as well as deepening faith and aware-ness of God's caring and attentive love — seeing the will of God expressed in human need especially the need people have for the basics of food, shelter, education, friendship, and encouragement. This gives a new dimension to the notion of priesthood in light of duties to one another.

I believe that my understanding of Jesuit vowed life and priesthood has taken its shape over the past eleven years influenced chiefly by my times of study both in philosophy and law, my work as a teacher both on the high school and college level, my efforts in Harlem, my legal work, my pres-ent theology studies and my new interest in spiritual direc-tion and retreat work. I understand the Jesuit vocation as a priestly one. The Formula makes that clear. I see my own particular vocation to the Jesuit priesthood as one that calls me to the works of preaching, teaching, giving the Spiritual Exercises, administering the sacraments, and working in the educational apostolate.

I look at Christ and see a servant model for priestly min-istry. Only when I take on the model of servant, as Christ did, can I minister to God's people the way I believe I have been called. My work in Harlem has taught me something about the poor, the broken, the oppressed. My legal work in Appalachia bas taught me to be concerned about unjust social structures. My eyes were opened to the scandal of an unjust state tax system when I worked on the Lincoln County (West Virginia) school case which resulted in a court ordered reform in the manner in which the state finances its schools as well as setting forth new educational standards throughout the West Virginia state school system.

The Final Word Is Love

We were just sitting there talking when Peter Maurin came in.

We were just sitting there talking when lines of people began to form, saying, "We need bread." We could not say, "Go, be thou filled." If there were six small loaves and a few fishes, we had to divide them. There was always bread.

We were just sitting there talking and people moved in on us. Let those who can take it, take it. Some moved out and that made room for more. And somehow the walls expanded.

We were just sitting there talking and someone said, "Let's all go live on a farm."

It was as casual as all that, I often think. It just came about. It just happened.

I found myself, a barren woman, the joyful mother of children. It is not always easy to be joyful, to keep in mind the duty of delight.

The most significant thing about The Catholic Worker is poverty, some say.

The most significant thing is community, others say. We are not alone any more.

But the final word is love. At times it has been, in the words of Father Zossima, a harsh and dreadful thing, and our very faith in love has been tried through fire.

We cannot love God unless we love each other, and to love we must know each other. We know Him in the breaking of bread, and we are not alone any more. Heaven is a banquet and life is a banquet, too, even with a crust, where there is companionship.

We have all known the long loneliness and we have learned that the only solution is love and that love comes with community.

It all happened while we sat there talking, and it is still going on.

The Dorothy Day Elementary School

Mission Statement

Draft

June 6, 2000

The mission of the Dorothy Day Elementary School is to provide an excellent Catholic education from K through 5th Grade for children in Southwest Baltimore City. Named for Dorothy Day and empowered by gospel values of justice and peace, this school seeks to create an educational environmental that serves, motivates and challenges urban children to educational, moral, and spiritual excellence. The Dorothy Day multi-cultural community in Southwest Baltimore and to prepare children from this community for admission to outstanding area high schools.

The Dorothy Day Elementary School Project Committee

Rev. Timothy Brown, S.J.
Sr. Mary Ann Hartnett, SSND

Rev. John Harvey, OFM.Cap.
Ms. Terry Huidobro
Mr. Joseph Molyneaux
Sr. Katherine Neuslein, RSM
Sr. Patricia Rogucki, SFCC
Ms. Kate Walsh-Little

Dorothy Day Academy

Evolution of the School

The Dorothy Day Academy arose out of a dire need for an alternative Catholic elementary school in southwest Baltimore. The crisis in the public school system prompted a small group of people from various places to discuss beginning a new school. After observing other neighborhoods and thinking of the population to be served, a group of teachers, clergy, and business people began meeting in the spring of 1999 to discuss plans for the new school. Those involved in the discussion and planning include: Fr. Tim Brown, Sr. Mary Anti Hartnett, Fr. John Harvey, Terry Huidobro, Joe Molyneaux, Sr. Katherine Neuslem, Sr. Patricia Rogucki, and Kate Walsh-Little.

The location of the school in southwest Baltimore was a logical choice since there are no other Catholic elementary schools in the area. It was agreed that Sowebo (Southwest Baltimore) is the area where the school should be located because there is the greatest need there. Catholic Community School and St. Bernadine's are in the neighboring communities of south Baltimore and west Baltimore respectively and serve students from those neighborhoods; thus, we would not interfere with any students who might attend those schools.

The name-the Dorothy Day Academy-reflects the values of peace and justice that we hope to instill in the students who attend and a vision of a more just world that can be created to meet everyone's needs. Dorothy Day was a prime example of a leader in social justice and is a role model for young people today. By incorporating the values of the Catholic Worker, we hope to teach students the importance of doing the Works of Mercy as well as raising questions about inequalities that exist in our society.

As the meetings for the school have progressed, we have explored different buildings to locate the school. A mission statement has been developed and job descriptions have been written. We are currently formulating a time line as well as establishing the school's governance. A liaison person will be determined to act as a point person with the Department of Education. We are still in the early stages of planning for the school, but our group is eagerly working to begin the Dorothy Day Academy as soon as possible.

Cultural Aspects of the Dorothy Day Academy

Dorothy Day was a great opera lover. She listened to the Metropolitan Opera every Saturday afternoon.

The Academy will place an emphasis on music, art, and literature.

One of my own mentors, Ned O'Gorman wrote a book about his own storefront school founded in the mid 1960s on Madison Avenue and 129th Street in New York's Harlem neighborhood. He writes in the introduction "Childhood is a gift the gods give children. It is as precious as the rubies they give the earth and the sun they give the spheres. It is each child's absolutely; as rare as a unicorn or a phoenix. One childhood to every child. No two child-hoods are alike. Childhood is the form that upholds each child's life forever. (p.3)

O'Gorman goes on to observe the mystical element of childhood. All children are mystics from his point of view. But there are, he adds, many who make it their work to drive the mystic out of the child.

Exploring his pedagogy and linking it to the spirituality of Dorothy Day, I see amazing connections.

O'Gorman notes the "child's kinship to the world is direct, silent, secret, wandering, and fearless. A child is a mystic because he sees whatever is around him as if he (she) were it. (p. 31)

What a marvelous introduction to prayer and contemplative living that can happen when a child is introduced to the loving, holy, mystical wisdom of Dorothy Day.

In her notebooks, Day wrote a great deal about the contemplative life. Some observations:

1. The main point in the contemplative life is looking at God and his truth, the thing all human existence is directed towards.

2. The contemplative life, then, has a second component: the investigation of nature, the world and whatever derives from God. Another way to come to know God! To quote Augustine, "When you set out to acquaint yourself with the natural wonders science disclosed, don't flit from one fact to another just to satisfy your curiosity, but carefully penetrate the various levels of reality until you come to the permanent and the eternal!"

—We need to feast on beauty to refresh ourselves and to remember Dostoyevsky's wonderful words "The world will be saved by beauty."

Dorothy's Spirituality

In the book Praying with Dorothy Day, the authors summarize the key characteristics of Dorothy Day's spirituality.

These key characteristics serve to form the philosophical basis for the Dorothy Day Academy.

Dorothy Day's spirituality is marked by:
1.   Solidarity with the poor.
2.   Her writings – Direct practice of works of mercy, and her own voluntary poverty bound her to poor, homeless, sick, and desperate people.
3.   Personalism – Dorothy loved doing works of mercy because they allowed her to take direct and immediate action for her brothers and sisters in Christ against the evils of society that robbed them of their life, freedom, and dignity.
4.   Prophetic Witness – By her public words and work, Dorothy sought to imitate Christ's witness against injustice, even when such witness seemed folly.
5.   Peacemaking – A steadfast pacifist, Dorothy opposed all wars and the use of violence to

solve human problems. She practiced and promoted human dignity with the spiritual weapons of prayer, fasting, almsgiving, civil disobedience, and works of amendment.

6.   A Sacramental sense – Dorothy looked to sacramental celebrations, especially the Eucharist, for daily spiritual sustenance.

7.   Gratitude – In good times and in bad, Dorothy had a keen sense of appreciation and learned to trust in the providence of God.

In Shaping School Culture: the Heart of Leadership, Terrence Deal speaks about the cultural aspects that signify a good school setting. He speaks of the importance of rituals, myths, storytelling, ceremony, symbolic meanings, metaphors, legends, and traditions as ways to communicate the values and principles of a school's mission. There is a need for a unique cultural tapestry as a means to commu¬nicate the message of education to young students. Deal defines culture as "the web of significance in which we are all suspended." (p-4)

I envision the Dorothy Day Academy as a place where the Gospel values as interpreted through Dorothy's life can come alive through a distinct and clear-cut philosophical mission statement.

Some of the tenets of The Catholic Worker movement help to flesh out that mission statement making it come alive in the hallways, classrooms, and playgrounds of the Academy.

Some of those cultural tenets include the following Catholic Worker Principles

The Duty of Hospitality – We are called to be Ambassadors of God.

The Human approach to life – To give and not to take is what makes us human; To serve and not to rule is what makes us human; To help and not to crush is what makes us human.

Scripture

In 1976 Dorothy reflected on the role of the Scriptures and specifically the Psalms in her daily life. She writes in the October 1976 Catholic Worker:

"All the Thursday Psalms are Psalms of Rejoicing. One line of a psalm is 'Be still and know that I am God.' You hear things in your own silences. The beauty of nature, the sound of waves, the sound of insects, the cicadas in the trees — all were part of my joy in nature that brought to the Church. I don't think we can over-emphasize the importance of song. Psalm 96 begins: 'Sing to the Lord a new song. Sing joyfully to the Lord, all you lands; break into song; sing praise. Let the sea and what fills it resound, the world and those who dwell in it. Let the rivers clap their hands, the mountains shout with them for joy.'"

I envision a school where children are taught to sing the psalms – to praise God each day perhaps a version of the daily office could be incorporated in morning prayer – a chapel choir formed.

Students could be introduced to musical instruments at an early age. They could begin to sing in choir and learn musical instruments to accompany the voices. I envision a morning time in chapel to begin the day praising God, listening to the Gospel of the day and having time to reflect and pray.

One them could be a centering prayer service once a week to help focus the students day.

Centering Prayer at the Dorothy Day Academy involves four aspects:

1. Choosing a sacred word as the symbol of the week. Given all the values of peacemaking, non-violence, Gospel values and appreciation for creation-a number of themes could develop over the academic year.

2. One teacher could introduce the word and ask that the students sit quietly with that word for a few minutes.

3. After a few minutes the teacher could reflect on the meaning of that word -possibly a fruit of the Holy Spirit Kindness, understanding, compassion, patience — for example

4. At the end of the prayer session the students could pray for a few minutes with daily intentions.

A Room for Christ

It is no use to say that we are born two thousand years too late to give room to Christ. Nor will those who live at the end of the world have been born too late. Christ is always with us, always asking for room in our hearts.

But now it is with the voice of our contemporaries that He speaks, with the eyes of store clerks, factory workers and children that He gazes; with the hands of office workers, slum dwellers and suburban housewives that He gives. It is with the feet of soldiers and tramps that He walks, and with the heart of anyone in need that He longs for shelter. And giving shelter or food to anyone who asks for it, or needs it, is giving it to Christ.

…All that the friends of Christ did for Him in his lifetime, we can do. Peter's mother-in-law hastened to cook a meal for Him, and if anything in the Gospels can be inferred, it surely is that she gave the very best she had, with no thought of extravagance. Matthew made a feast for Him, inviting the whole town, so that the house was in an uproar of enjoyment, and the straight-laced Pharisees—the good people—were scandalized.

The people of Samaria, despised and isolated, were over-joyed to give Him hospitality, and for days He walked and ate and slept among them. And the loveliest of all relationships in Christ's life, after His relationship with his Mother, is His friendship with Martha, Mary and Lazarus and the continual hospitality He found with them. It is a staggering thought that there were once two sisters and a brother whom Jesus looked on almost as His family and where He found a second home…

If we hadn't got Christ's own words for it, it would seem raving lunacy to believe that if I offer a bed and food and hospitality to some man or woman or child, I am replaying the part of Lazarus or Martha or Mary, and that my guest is Christ. There is nothing to show it, perhaps. There are no haloes already glowing round their heads–at least none that human eyes can see…

We can do it too, exactly as they did. We are not born too late. We do it by seeing Christ and serving Christ in friends and strangers, in everyone we come in contact with…

…He said that a glass of water given to a beggar was given to Him. He made heaven hinge on the way we act towards Him in His disguise of commonplace, frail and ordinary humanity…

And to those who say, aghast, that they never had a chance to do such a thing, that they lived two thousand years too late, He will say again what they had the chance of knowing all their lives, that if these things were done for the very least of his brethren they were done for Him.

—Dorothy Day

Blowing the Dynamite

Writing about the Catholic Church,
a radical writer says:
"Rome will have to do more
than to play a waiting game;
she will have to use
some of the dynamite
inherent in her message."
To blow the dynamite
of a message
is the only way
to make the message dynamic.
If the Catholic Church
is not today
the dominant social dynamic force,
it is because Catholic scholars
have failed to blow the dynamite
of the Church.
Catholic scholars
have taken the dynamite
of the Church,
have wrapped it up
in nice phraseology,
placed it in an hermetic container

and sat on the lid.
It is about time
to blow the lid off
so the Catholic Church
may again become
the dominant social dynamic force.

—Peter Maurin

Big Shots and Little Shots

America is all shot to pieces
  since the little shots
  are no longer able
  to become big shots.

When the little shots
  are not satisfied
  to remain little shots
  and try to become big shots,
  then the big shots
  are not satisfied
  to remain big shots
  and try to become bigger shots.

And when the big shots
  become bigger shots
  then the little shots
  become littler shots.

And when the little shots
  become littler shots
  because the big shots
  become bigger shots

then the little shots
get mad at the big shots.
And when the little shots
  get mad at the big shots
  because the big shots
  by becoming bigger shots
  make the little shots
  littler shots
  they shoot the big shots
  full of little shots.

But by shooting the big shots
  full of little shots
  the little shots
  do not become big shots;
  they make everything all shot.

And I don't like
  to see the little shots
  shoot the big shots
  full of little shots;
  that is why
  I am trying to shoot
  both the big shots
  and the little shots
  full of hot shots.

—Peter Maurin

Long Loneliness

We have always acknowledged the primacy of the spiritual, and to have undertaken a life of silence, manual labor and prayer might have been the better way. But I do not know. God gave us our temperaments, and in spite of my pacifism, it is natural for me to stand my ground, to continue in what actually amounts to a class war, using such weapons as the works of mercy for immediate means to show our love and to alleviate suffering.

And the weapons of journalism! My whole life had been in journalism and I saw the world in terms of class conflict. I did not look upon class war as something to be stirred up, as the Marxist did. I did not want to increase what was already there but to mitigate it. When we were invited to help during a strike, we went to perform the works of mercy, which include not only feeding the hungry, visiting the imprisoned, but enlightening the ignorant and rebuking the unjust. We were ready to "endure wrongs patiently" for ourselves (this is another of the spiritual works of mercy) but we were not going to be meek for others, enduring their wrongs patiently...

Peter used to say when we covered strikes and joined picket lines, "Strikes don't strike me." Yet he took the occasion to come out on the picket line to distribute leaflets upon which some single point was made. "To change the hearts and minds of men," he said. "To give them vision—the vision of a society where it is easier for men to be good."

—*Long Loneliness*

Part 4

To Collaborate in the Care
of Our Common Home

In Chapter Four of *Laudato Si'*, Pope Francis stresses that everything is interconnected in the web of life. With renewed vigor, he calls for a preferential option for the poor and disenfranchised throughout the world, who often bear the brunt of our disconnected society. He also says that technological solutions to environmental issues must respect the "rights of peoples and cultures" around the globe.

1. Pope Francis says: "It cannot be emphasized enough how everything is interconnected. Time and space are not independent of one another, and not even atoms or subatomic particles can be considered in isolation." What are some examples of the "interconnectedness" of the universe that you have experienced in your own life? How does seeing everything as connected change the way you see the world?

2. "Lack of respect for the law is becoming more common," we read. Do you agree or disagree?

3. Pope Francis says, "Ecology, then, also involves protecting the cultural treasures of humanity in the broadest sense." What link do you see between protecting cultural treasures and ecology? Are there examples you can think of from current news?

4. In what ways must technological solutions to environmental issues need to respect the "rights of peoples and cultures"? Why is

the loss of human culture as serious as the extinction of plants and animals?

5. "Learning to accept our body, to care for it and to respect its fullest meaning, is an essential element of any genuine human ecology," Pope Francis says. Have you considered that how you take care of your body has repercussion on the world at large? How can you become a better caretaker of your own body?

A prayer for our earth

All-powerful God, you are present in the whole universe
  and in the smallest of your creatures.
You embrace with your tenderness all that exists.
Pour out upon us the power of your love,
that we may protect life and beauty.

Fill us with peace, that we may live
as brothers and sisters, harming no one.
O God of the poor,
help us to rescue the abandoned and forgotten of this
  earth,
so precious in your eyes.
Bring healing to our lives,
that we may protect the world and not prey on it,
that we may sow beauty, not pollution and destruction.
Touch the hearts
of those who look only for gain
at the expense of the poor and the earth.
Teach us to discover the worth of each thing,
to be filled with awe and contemplation,
to recognize that we are profoundly united
with every creature
as we journey towards your infinite light.

We thank you for being with us each day.
Encourage us, we pray, in our struggle
for justice, love and peace.

Noah's Prayer

Lord,
what a menagerie!
Between Your downpour and these animal cries
one cannot hear oneself think!
The days are long,
Lord.
All this water makes my heart sink.
When will the ground cease to rock under my feet?
The days are long.
Master Raven has not come back.
Here is Your dove.
Will she find us a twig of hope?
The days are long,
Lord.
Guide Your Ark to safety,
some zenith of rest,
where we can escape at last
from this brute slavery.
The days are long,
Lord.
Lead me until I reach the shore of Your covenant.
Amen.

—Prayers from the Ark
Carmen Bernos de Gasztold

LAUDATO SI'

II. THE WISDOM OF THE BIBLICAL ACCOUNTS

65. Without repeating the entire theology of creation, we can ask what the great biblical narratives say about the relationship of human beings with the world. In the first creation account in the Book of Genesis, God's plan includes creating humanity. After the creation of man and woman, "God saw everything that he had made, and behold it was very good" (Gen 1:31). The Bible teaches that every man and woman is created out of love and made in God's image and likeness (cf. Gen 1:26). This shows us the immense dignity of each person, "who is not just something, but someone. He is capable of self-knowledge, of self-possession and of freely giving himself and entering into communion with other persons". Saint John Paul II stated that the special love of the Creator for each human being "confers upon him or her an infinite dignity". Those who are committed to defending human dignity can find in the Christian faith the deepest reasons for this commitment. How wonderful is the certainty that each human life is not adrift in the midst of hopeless chaos, in a world ruled by pure chance or

endlessly recurring cycles! The Creator can say to each one of us: "Before I formed you in the womb, I knew you" (Jer 1:5). We were conceived in the heart of God, and for this reason "each of us is the result of a thought of God. Each of us is willed, each of us is loved, each of us is necessary".

——Encyclical Letter
Laudato Si' of the Holy Father Francis
On Care for Our Common Home

The Prayer of the Parrot

Did you say something
Lord?
Oh! I thought
You were speaking to me.
You are silent?
Are You afraid
I shall tell
Your secrets?
It's true
I'm a little talkative
but, at times,
that is useful:
heads are thick,
slow to understand,
and have to be told things
again and again.
If You need me,
I am Your servant,
one who never grows tired
repeating the same word
again and again,
which has its power:
I may grow tedious

but people listen
in spite of themselves;
and what is repeated,
repeated, repeated,
stays in the memory.
When may I serve
Your infinite wisdom?
Think of it, Lord

—Prayers from the Ark
Carmen Bernos de Gasztold

LAUDATO SI'

IV. THE MESSAGE OF EACH CREATURE IN THE HARMONY OF CREATION

84. Our insistence that each human being is an image of God should not make us overlook the fact that each creature has its own purpose. None is superfluous. The entire material universe speaks of God's love, his boundless affection for us. Soil, water, mountains: everything is, as it were, a caress of God. The history of our friendship with God is always linked to particular places which take on an intensely personal meaning; we all remember places, and revisiting those memories does us much good. Anyone who has grown up in the hills or used to sit by the spring to drink, or played outdoors in the neighborhood square; going back to these places is a chance to recover something of their true selves.

—Encyclical Letter
Laudato Si' of the Holy Father Francis
On Care for Our Common Home

The Prayer of the Dog

Lord,
I keep watch!
If I am not here
who will guard their house?
Watch over their sheep?
Be faithful?
No one but You and I
understands
what faithfulness is.
They call me, "Good dog! Nice dog!"
Words…
I take their pats
and the old bones they throw me
and I seem pleased.
They really believe they make me happy.
I take kicks too
when they come my way.
None of that matters.
I keep watch!

Lord,
do not let me die
until, for them,
all danger is driven away.

Amen.

—Prayers from the Ark
Carmen Bernos de Gasztold

LAUDATO SI'

85. God has written a precious book, "whose letters are the multitude of created things present in the universe". The Canadian bishops rightly pointed out that no creature is excluded from this manifestation of God: "From panoramic vistas to the tiniest living form, nature is a constant source of wonder and awe. It is also a continuing revelation of the divine". The bishops of Japan, for their part, made a thought-provoking observation: "To sense each creature singing the hymn of its existence is to live joyfully in God's love and hope". This contemplation of creation allows us to discover in each thing a teaching which God wishes to hand on to us, since "for the believer, to contemplate creation is to hear a message, to listen to a paradoxical and silent voice". We can say that "alongside revelation properly so-called, contained in sacred Scripture, there is a divine manifestation in the blaze of the sun and the fall of night". Paying attention to this manifestation, we learn to see ourselves in relation to all other creatures: "I express myself in expressing the world; in my effort to decipher the sacredness of the world, I explore my own".

—Encyclical Letter
Laudato Si' of the Holy Father Francis
On Care for Our Common Home

The Prayer of the Litle Pig

Lord,
their politeness makes me laugh!
Yes, I grunt!
Grunt and snuffle!
I grunt because I grunt
and snuffle
because I cannot do anything else!
All the same, I am not going to thank them
for fattening me up to make bacon.
Why did You make me so tender?
What a fate!
Lord,
teach me how to say

Amen

—Prayers from the Ark
Carmen Bernos de Gasztold

LAUDATO SI'

87. When we can see God reflected in all that exists, our hearts are moved to praise the Lord for all his creatures and to worship him in union with them. This sentiment finds magnificent expression in the hymn of Saint Francis of Assisi:

Praised be you, my Lord, with all your creatures,
especially Sir Brother Sun,
who is the day and through whom you give us light.
And he is beautiful and radiant with great splendor;
and bears a likeness of you, Most High.
Praised be you, my Lord, through Sister Moon and the
*   stars,*
in heaven you formed them clear and precious and
*   beautiful.*
Praised be you, my Lord, through Brother Wind,
and through the air, cloudy and serene, and every kind of
*   weather*
through whom you give sustenance to your creatures.
Praised be you, my Lord, through Sister Water,
who is very useful and humble and precious and chaste.
Praised be you, my Lord, through Brother Fire,

through whom you light the night,
and he is beautiful and playful and robust and strong".

—Encyclical Letter
Laudato Si' of the Holy Father Francis
On Care for Our Common Home

The Prayer of the Raven

I believe,
Lord,
I believe!
It is faith that saves us, You have said it!
I believe the world was made for me,
because as it dies
I thrive on it.
My undertaker's black
is in keeping with my cynical old heart.
Raven land is between You
and that life down there, for whose end I wait
to gratify myself.
"Aha!" I cry. "Avant moi le deluge!"
What a feast!
I shall never go back to the Ark!
To the Ark…
Oh! let it die in me—
this horrible nostalgia.

Amen.

—Prayers from the Ark
Carmen Bernos de Gasztold

LAUDATO SI'

92. Moreover, when our hearts are authentically open to universal communion, this sense of fraternity excludes nothing and no one. It follows that our indifference or cruelty towards fellow creatures of this world sooner or later affects the treatment we mete out to other human beings. We have only one heart, and the same wretchedness which leads us to mistreat an animal will not be long in showing itself in our relationships with other people. Every act of cruelty towards any creature is "contrary to human dignity". We can hardly consider ourselves to be fully loving if we disregard any aspect of reality: "Peace, justice and the preservation of creation are three absolutely interconnected themes, which cannot be separated and treated individually without once again falling into reductionism". Everything is related, and we human beings are united as brothers and sisters on a wonderful pilgrimage, woven together by the love God has for each of his creatures and which also unites us in fond affection with brother sun, sister moon, brother river and mother earth.

—Encyclical Letter
Laudato Si' of the Holy Father Francis
On Care for Our Common Home

The Prayer of the Elephant

Dear God,
it is I, the elephant,
Your creature,
who is talking to You.
I am so embarrassed by my great self,
and truly it is not my fault
if I spoil Your jungle a little with my big feet.
Let me be careful and behave wisely,
always keeping my dignity and poise.
Give me such philosophic thoughts
that I can rejoice everywhere I go
in the lovable oddity of things.

Amen.

—Prayers from the Ark
Carmen Bernos de Gasztold

Sustainable Communities: Appalachia

Pastoral Message

In this letter we wish to explore
the new tasks which lie before us
particularly the task of creating or defending
what are called
"sustainable communities"
These are communities where people and nature
can live together in harmony
and not rob from future generations.

Many thoughtful people worry that
in the post-industrial age
Appalachia will no longer be sustainable
they fear that Appalachia may become
a place only for

- large scale unemployment;
- the death of small local business;
- clear-cutting the forests;
- dumping out-of-state garbage;

- even dumping toxic radioactive materials;
- and warehousing prisoners from the cities.

In this unsustainable path for the future
Appalachia would become a waste-land.
If this path were to be followed
the local people and the local ecology
would be devastated.

Broader Implications

We do not see this conflict
between a culture of death and a culture of life
as simply an Appalachian crisis
Rather we see the Appalachia crisis
as a window into a larger- crisis
which now threatens the entire society
including the middle class
and indeed the full ecosystem
across the entire planet.

In response to this ancient message
we believe that we are still called:

- to defend Earth and the poor together,
- to learn from the wisdom of both;
- to care for God's single web of life.

In these tasks
the land and the people of Appalachia
are once again a precious gift to us all

Qver millions of years
where the Ice Age never reached,
winds and rains softened these mountains
made them more round and gentle
and carved within them
so many valleys and coves
and ridges and hollows.

To dwell within these mountains
is to experience:

- in their height, God's majesty
- in their weight God's strength
- in their hollows God's embrace
- in their waters God's cleansing
- in their haze God's mystery

These mountains are truly a holy place.

So too with the plants of this forest.

Here there flourishes
one of the richest bio-systems in the world.
Indeed the woods are full of
medicinal plants and glorious flowers.

We recall especially:

- mountain laurels and rhododendrons,
- azaleas and mountain magnolias,
- blossoms on tulip poplars and black locusts
- ginseng and yellow root.

Perhaps 3,000 to 4,000 years ago
the native peoples developed agriculture.
They grew corn and beans
and pumpkins and squash.
But they still journeyed to the mountains
for hunting and trade.

The original European settlers
often Scots-Irish,
brought their own gifts to the mountains.
We still love their Keltic melodies,
as well as folk instruments like the fiddle
And we still admire their crafts
particularly their stunning quilts.
These early settlers carried
an ancient "green" Keltic spirituality
rooted in the beauty of God's creation.

The freed African slave
also brought their rich spirituality:

- echoing in the rhythm of the drum
    the maternal heartbeat of all creation;
- singing great songs of faith and praise
    to celebrate the wonder of all creation;
    proclaiming in magnificent preaching
- God's own majestic word.

With new highways it was hoped that
"development" would come to the region
But by and large "development" did not come
And now so many good people
find themselves without work
The post-industrial crisis was already starting

But large super-stores did come to Appalachia
They brought new consumer goods
but unfortunately they also often

undermined rooted businesses
drained capital over from the region
weakened local government
bled resources from smaller rural towns

They also fostered the modern consumer society
the very opposite of Appalachia's old traditions
of artistic simplicity and creative crafts

These same remote rural areas
have also been identified
as places for countless new prisons,

where human beings from distant cities
themselves filled with unemployment
are being dumped off
as if they were social waste

Meanwhile local governments
again, especially in remote rural counties
are being tempted to depend for revenues
on the dumping of out-of-state waste
or else on new prisons
as the only way of creating jobs

At a Crossroads

Because across so many Appalachian counties
this unsuitable economics

now threatens both natural and social ecology,
the region stands at a historical crossroads.

That very idea
that economics should threaten
both natural and social ecology
is a contradiction.

For the word "economics"
comes from the Greek oikos and nomos,
which together mean "ordering of the home."
Similarly the word "ecology"

comes from the Greek oikos and logos,
which together mean "logic of the home"

How can economics and ecology,
as the "logic and order of the home"
be mutually opposed?
For the "home" is only one place.

As we enter this dangerous transition,
it is now clear that the industrial working class
and much of the corporate middle class
are, as they say, "downwardly mobile."
Jobs are disappearing and income is falling.

It is also clear that in American society
in terms of wealth as well as income,
the top has been gaining
and the bottom has been losing.

And again, at the intimate level,
tragically those who are victimized
sometimes fall prey to rage and despair,
and sometimes wrongly express their anger
in crimes against themselves and others,
and in violence against women and children.

In one path, which is not sustainable,
Appalachia will be devastated
by uprooted outside capital
and by uprooted inappropriate technologies,

unaccountable to local communities
and converting people and nature
into waste from the consumer society.

In the other path, which is sustainable,
the people and land of Appalachia,
using their own rich gifts
in social and ecological cooperation,
and taking advantage of
the new tools of the electronic age,
will form authentic local communities
rooted in God's sacred web of life.

In our regional hearings,
we could not help but feel people's deep anxiety,
as they face this crossroads
Countless folks told us about their worries:

- lack of good jobs,
- smaller, paychecks in remaining jobs,
- large amounts of unemployment,
- a harder time making ends meet,
- young people having to leave the region,
- people in their prime despairing,
- lack of health care,
- local businesses closing
- whole towns dying,
- great pressures on families,
- increased drug and alcohol abuse,
- violence against women and children,

- more crime, murder, and suicide,
- abandonment of families,
- the elderly being left alone,
- contamination of the waters,
- pollution in the mountain haze,
- flooding in the hollows after erosion,
- acid rain in the high altitudes,
- and so much more.

To this we add our own worries that,
as the social and ecological crisis increases,
a new selfishness spreads across the land,
and not only in Appalachia
We see this more broadly in:

- abandonment of the poor,
- increase of racism and scapegoating,
- demands for more and more guns,
- growing use of the death-penalty,
- campaigns for abortion and euthanasia,
- regional wars across the planet

One main reason for these worries
is that we are now experiencing:

- the death of the modern industrial age, and
- the birth of a postmodern electronic age,

Sustainable Communities

The Spirit of God is always active in history
bringing forth from emptiness and chaos
ever fresh creativity.

We call these new ways
the path of sustainable communities.
These are communities which will:

- conserve and not waste
- be simpler but better
- keep most resources circulating locally
- create sustainable livelihoods,
- support family life
- protect the richness of nature
- develop people spiritually
- and follow God's values.

Sustainable Forestry

Since Appalachia is basically forest
one of the most precious gifts
which God has given to the people
is the forest itself.

In this model there is no clear cutting.
Mature timber is selectively harvested

while the forest itself is sustained
in all its biodiversity.
In addition there is great care
in the felling of cut trees,
so as not to damage the remaining ones.
Then the logger cuts the tree into logs
while still in the forest
and even uses draft horses
to pull the logs out,
so as not to damage the forest.
Ideally the logs are dried locally
by means of a solar kiln.

In this model of forestry
the crop lasts forever
and the forest's biodiversity remains intact.
It is important to remember here
that the forest is more than the trees.
It is a whole bio-system
with countless life forms
all of which form an ecosystem.

Sustainable Families

Sometimes our local communities
are devastated from the outside,
but sometimes they are also
devastated from the inside—

in the very soul.

Perhaps the worst internal devastation
of local families and communities
comes from domestic violence,
This is not simply an Appalachian problem,
but a problem of the whole world.
Families often become unsustainable
when people lose their sense of self-worth,
particularly when they are out of work,
or under great hardship.

Clearly the present economic crisis,
not only in Appalachia but around the world,
is for many individuals and families
one of those moments of great hardship.

In this difficult social context,
there arises the terrible temptation
for family members to take it out on each other,
often with husbands battering wives.
and often with parents abusing children.

Often driving such violence are
destructive addictions to:

- the abuse of alcohol,
- the abuse of drugs,
- the abuse of sex.

Through an addiction,
a person tries to gain power,
but it is not a life-giving power.
Rather all addictions reveal
the destructive face of sin.

Addictions block a person's creativity,
by repressing the image of God.
Instead they make the person serve an idol,
and then point the addicted individuals,
and sometimes those around them,
slowly towards death.

We also know that addictions
are often accompanied by
what are called codependences.
Where the addict seeks abusive power
the codependent rejects good self-power
claiming to be completely helpless.
Here too there is
a disfiguration of the image of God
deep within the soul.

But we trust in Jesus healing love.
And so we know that
these great wounds can be healed.
To help wounded families to find healing
and to become emotionally sustainable
we need prayer and forgiveness

but not a false forgiveness
which covers up the problem.

For loving forgiveness
must always be based on truth.
To live the truth in love
we need personal and family supports
rooted in the local community.

Much More to Say
These are only some
of the experiments and ideas
presently being explored in Appalachia.
Once again we praise them
as creative seed of a new civilization
serving the web of life.

There are other great needs too,
and no doubt other important experiments
also responding to these needs.
Here we think of the many young people
who have been forced to emigrate
out of the mountains to the cities.
We wish to point out the need
for church organizations to serve migrants
in the cities where they have gone.

We also think of holistic health care,
and, in addition of creative education,
as pressing needs of local communities,

But there is not space here
adequately to address all these issues.

—Catholic Committee of Appalachia
Dickinson County, Virginia

About the Author

Father Timothy Brown, S.J. is an Associate Professor of Law and Social Responsibility and Assistant to the President for Mission Integration. In his role, Fr. Brown develops numerous mission-focused programs to promote the Catholic and Jesuit nature of the University, including offering the Spiritual Exercises. Fr. Brown first came to Loyola in 1987 and has served as a faculty member in The Sellinger School of Business and Management and currently teaches classes in Legal Environment of Business; Messina Criminal Law; Race and the Law; and Speech Writing and Delivery. Other classes include Sports Law; Constitutional Law; Ignatian Spirituality and the Law; and First Amendment in the age of Trump. Honors for his teaching include the Sellinger School Overall Outstanding Faculty Award, the Harry W. Rodgers Distinguished Teacher of the Year award, and the Educator for Life Award. In 2023, Fr. Brown founded The Rev. Timothy Brown, S.J. Ignatian Life Center as the organizational locus for the promotion of the Jesuit and Ignatian spiritual tradition at Loyola University Maryland and is in service to the Baltimore community. A former provincial for the Maryland Province of the Society of Jesus, Fr. Brown earned his B.S. from Georgetown, M.A. from Fordham, M.Div. from the Weston School of University, and his J.D. from George Mason University. He serves on the Archdiocese of Baltimore School Board and the board for Cristo Rey Jesuit High School in Baltimore.

Apprentice
House Press
Loyola University Maryland

Apprentice House is the country's only campus-based, student-staffed book publishing company. Directed by professors and industry professionals, it is a nonprofit activity of the Communication Department at Loyola University Maryland.

Using state-of-the-art technology and an experiential learning model of education, Apprentice House publishes books in untraditional ways. This dual responsibility as publishers and educators creates an unprecedented collaborative environment among faculty and students, while teaching tomorrow's editors, designers, and marketers.

Eclectic and provocative, Apprentice House titles intend to entertain as well as spark dialogue on a variety of topics. Financial contributions to sustain the press's work are welcomed. Contributions are tax deductible to the fullest extent allowed by the IRS.

To learn more about Apprentice House books or to obtain submission guidelines, please visit www.apprenticehouse.com.

Apprentice House Press
Communication Department
Loyola University Maryland
4501 N. Charles Street
Baltimore, MD 21210
Ph: 410-617-5265
info@apprenticehouse.com • www.apprenticehouse.com